YOUR KNOWLEDGE HAS VALUE

- We will publish your bachelor's and master's thesis, essays and papers

- Your own eBook and book - sold worldwide in all relevant shops

- Earn money with each sale

Upload your text at www.GRIN.com and publish for free

Bibliographic information published by the German National Library:

The German National Library lists this publication in the National Bibliography; detailed bibliographic data are available on the Internet at http://dnb.dnb.de .

This book is copyright material and must not be copied, reproduced, transferred, distributed, leased, licensed or publicly performed or used in any way except as specifically permitted in writing by the publishers, as allowed under the terms and conditions under which it was purchased or as strictly permitted by applicable copyright law. Any unauthorized distribution or use of this text may be a direct infringement of the author s and publisher s rights and those responsible may be liable in law accordingly.

Imprint:

Copyright © 2019 GRIN Verlag
Print and binding: Books on Demand GmbH, Norderstedt Germany
ISBN: 9783668914070

This book at GRIN:

https://www.grin.com/document/461247

Dennis Sui

The multifaced dyscalculia. Cognitive bases, diagnostics and learning intervention

GRIN Verlag

GRIN - Your knowledge has value

Since its foundation in 1998, GRIN has specialized in publishing academic texts by students, college teachers and other academics as e-book and printed book. The website www.grin.com is an ideal platform for presenting term papers, final papers, scientific essays, dissertations and specialist books.

Visit us on the internet:

http://www.grin.com/

http://www.facebook.com/grincom

http://www.twitter.com/grin_com

The multifaced dyscalculia:
cognitive bases, diagnostics and learning intervention.

Abstract: Dyscalculia is an interesting researcher topic in many aspects. This impairment of counting abilities, which according to various estimates is subject to 5-12 percent of the population, has loudly declared itself in the last 10-15 years due to obvious importance of mathematical abilities in modern society. It turned out that the impairment has a multiple nature and multiple manifestations. The largest number of studies has been related to children's education. The problems of early diagnosis and pedagogical intervention have attracted special attention of researchers. The article provides an overview of the basic knowledge of the impairment at the moment, focuses on practice-oriented concepts, highlights the techniques of Western pedagogies.

The answer to the question "What is mathematics?", is "Mathematics is mathematical thinking". And what is mathematical thinking? It is a conceptual structure based on a multitude of links between mathematical relationships, mathematical rules and laws, and mathematical operations [Case, 1992]. Everyday math includes counting (reciting the number words, knowing their order), reading and writing numerals and their arithmetical combinations (knowing the meaning of symbols), understanding number magnitudes (distinguish more from less), retrieving number facts (e.g. 2x2=4), turn to principles, concepts and laws (e.g. multiplying by ten adds one zero, adding increases, dividing reduces etc.). Even the basic mathematical skills are crucial to meet the requirements of the society. All these skills have the notion of quantity in common. The very awareness that *something* can be *counted*. In some people's mind it may go wrong at a physical level, what leads to the phenomenon that is called dyscalculia.

At the heart of it is the inability to estimate "at a glance" (without recalculation) the number of objects in sets. Dyscalculia is a cognitive and behavioral impairment, forcing an adult to count his fingers at a cash register in a store, and a first grader to feel an outsider because he does not understand what everyone else can easily cope with. Until the teacher recognizes his inner inability and turns to modern correctional pedagogy the latter will having trouble building up his "multitude of links between mathematical relationships, mathematical rules and laws, and mathematical operations". Hence the former one never had the chance because of a much lower awareness of his teacher, as well as his parents, the educational system and the whole society.

They may have different manifestations, but they both have the same problem. Undeveloped structures of the cerebral cortex, first of all intraparietal sulcus – "the arithmetic organ of the brain", the area of the parietal cortex responsible for estimating the number of objects in the sets. It gets excited when performing any mental operations related to quantities and arithmetic, which confirms its central role in mathematical thinking. But it is more than just this part of the brain that belongs to the "arithmetic network". It also includes [Butterworth, Varma, Laurillard, 2011]: The prefrontal cortex (responsible for conscious rational activity, attention and working memory, is activated when confronted with new types of tasks), the angular gyrus of the left parietal lobe (extracting facts from long-term memory, solving familiar problems) as well as the fusiform gyrus (understanding symbols – words and numarals that denote numbers). This is also the reason why dyscalculia needs to be distinguished from math anxiety, which can seriously affect math results as well, but it is more an emotional rather than cognitive state involving activation of brain regions associated with fear and coping negative emotions [Young, Wu, Menon, 2012]. In children suffering from dyscalculia, when solving arithmetic problems, the intra-minor sulcus works less actively, and the gray matter volume in this part of the brain is less than in peers who do not have difficulties with arithmetic. In addition, it turned out that in dyscalculia, on average, neural connections between the fusiform gyrus and parietal lobes are less developed.

Early formation of such ligaments can be decisive for obtaining mathematical knowledge at an older age. Children who have not developed such relationships may subsequently need intervention to form them. Important is that children with dyscalculia still develop a consistent level of intelligence in other areas of learning and life. But nevertheless low math ability can lead to behavioral and emotional symptoms.

Therefore, complex and effective diagnosis and intervention strategies are necessary that take account of difference of the multitude of dyscalculia manifestations. In fact there are so many different faces of math abilities impairment, that during the last two decades depending on the test and criteria, a multitude of names was used, such as arithmetic-related learning disabilities (AD), arithmetical disability (ARITHD), arithmetic learning disability (ALD), mathematical disability (MD), mathematics learning disability (MLD), mathematical learning difficulty (MLD). The name dyscalculia or developmental dyscalculia is reserved for a deficit in core numerical abilities, whereas MLD for instance is the result of several general cognitive deficits such as deficient working memory, visual-spatial processing or attention.

There is no single approach that could instantly diagnose dyscalculia. Nevertheless, typologies of functional deviations are proposed. There is a four factors model to determine the basic mathematical abilities in the age group of 5-8 years [Geary, 2012]: non-verbal and symbolic arithmetic thinking; knowledge of numbers; basic counting and arithmetic skills and understanding of mathematical relationships.

The founders of the concept of "positive arithmetic thinking" [Okamoto & Case, 1996; Kalchman, Moss, & Case, 2001] include in the structure of this concept: a) fluency of estimates and judgments about magnitudes; b) the ability to recognize results as unfounded; c) flexibility in mental calculations; d) the ability to navigate the system of representations and choose the most appropriate. It is stated that in children of preschool age, the two key components of arithmetic thinking are not quite strongly connected with each other and are, rather, prototypes of other components of arithmetic thinking are the ability to evaluate (judgments) and the ability to navigate in the system of representations.

Three relatively compact evaluation parameters are also very promising: a) quantity discrimination, or magnitude comparison; b) identification of a missing digit / number in a sequential series as a criterion for account knowledge; c) ability to identify numerals / numbers.

There is also a more systematic view on the impairment and its diagnosis. In fact one of the first researchers of dyscalculia L. Kosc proposed his classification of deficit profiles [Kosc, 1974]:

1. Verbal dyscalculia, implying a violation of the verbal designation of mathematical concepts, i.e. the student finds it difficult to name numbers, symbols, quantities, mathematical concepts, it is difficult to perform the conversion operation, but computational operations can be performed quite successfully.

2. Dyslexic dyscalculia - impaired reading of mathematical signs, verbal designation of mathematical concepts. This type of dyscalculia is often combined with other types of inability to math and inability to learn in other aspects, such as dyslexia.

3. Graphic dyscalculia - a violation of the recording of mathematical symbols and the correct reproduction of geometric figures: it is difficult to designate the number of a verbally given number by a number, or to copy the written number.

4. Operational dyscalculia - inability to perform or accurately apply mathematical operations: the solutions found for mathematical problems are most often incorrect due to the erroneous application of mathematical operations. However, the correct decision is also random, since inadequate mathematical operations were used.

5. Spatial dyscalculia is characterized by difficulties arising for the student in perception or visual organization of arithmetic problems, for example, performing a computational action, the student ignores part of the task written on the right side of the paper.

6. Oligocalculia (generalized) is a common inability that causes the breakdown of a wide range of mathematical functions. Oligocalculia is often accompanied by mental retardation, while other types of dyscalculia can develop with a consistent level of intelligence.

7. Pseudo-dyscalculia is an underdevelopment of mathematical abilities resulting from lack of education, lack of motivation to study, academic lag or inadequacy of training programs and techniques.

This classification was well adopted by many countries and has emerged as an unconditional practical orientation and affordable monitoring and prevention tools [Ermolova, Ponomareva, Frolova, 2016].

The diagnose dyscalculia behavioral approach is used, based on analysing errors which includes implicit analysis of special features of space and time perception, visual-motor coordination, efficiency of memorization and information reproduction and processing, analytical and motivational components of cognitive behavior, math decision-making strategies, variability of behavioral response [Rysina, 2011]. It should be noted that erros are not noticed by children and are not corrected. Depending on the type of dyscalculia, the most common errors can be identified [Kairova, 2016]:

1. The unformedness of the concept of a natural number: they recalculate objects with violation of rules, as a result of this, they do not distinguish quantity as a common property of equal-power sets and do not realize that they got the same natural number as a result, and the number is called incorrectly. Children find it difficult to designate this number as a number, they do not recognize numbers, especially those having some of the same elements, do not establish a correspondence between a set of objects, a number characterizing this set, and a numeral to denote a number. In this regard, they do not establish a quantitative relationship between numbers, that is, they make mistakes when comparing numbers based on pairwise comparison of two sets of objects. Children experience even greater

difficulties in studying two-digit numbers: they do not recognize digits, they do not establish a decimal composition (structure) of a number, they do not realize the local value of a digit in a number record.

2. Unformed ideas about the properties of the natural series of numbers: they know the reference sequence of numbers, but they find it difficult to substantiate the place of a number in the natural series, in determining the "neighbors" of a named number, in highlighting the next and previous number relative to a given one, and how to get them (a- 1, a + 1); find it difficult to compare numbers based on the properties of the natural number.

3. The lack of formation of spatial representations in children: errors in writing the numbers ("drawing", "mirror writing"), orientation on the tutorial page is broken, "they do not see" the line in the notebook, they are not oriented in the written series of numbers, in the compiled addition, subtraction tables, multiplication and division; do not recognize familiar mathematical objects, if they are presented in any unusual perspective; do not perceive the expanded records of computational techniques.

4. Multiple computational errors: due to the incompleteness of the skill of tabular computation and difficulty in using tables to find the result for a long time, it is difficult to assimilate extra-tabular computation methods: improper simplification of computations, incorrect transfer of individual computational operations to a new situation, partial execution of calculations.

5. Unformed mathematical speech: do not distinguish terms and do not use them in speech or use them in an unusual sense, do not recognize mathematical signs and find it difficult to read mathematical records using

mathematical symbols and perform mathematical records (for example, when translating a specific situation into the language of symbols and signs, which is the main skill in solving a textual problem and in mastering the objective meaning of arithmetic operations).

6. The activity of a junior schoolchild with dyscalculia in solving a textual problem is uncontrolled, chaotic.

The key to intervention of dyscalculia is neuroplasticity. Underdeveloped areas of the brain can be developed by hard training, about the same as muscles. With appropriate and specific intervention provided, children with dyscalculia can succeed at acquiring the basic number concepts needed for math learning, greatly impacting the affective domain of children, raising self-esteem and developing a more positive attitude to the learning of mathematics [Zerafa, 2015]. Available neurobiological data can make the intervention of teachers and psychologists more targeted. Modern research indicates the efficacy of theory-based, individually-tailored neuropsychological rehabilitation [De Nigris, Anna & Masciarelli, Giovanni & Guariglia, Cecilia, 2019], neuroplasticity trainig makes it possible to rebuild deteriorated brain functions and help affected children to develop new brain strategies to compensate dyscalculia. [Garcia-Camba, Maria & Garcia Planas, Maria Isabel, 2018].

A multifaced impairment needs a multifunctional therapy [e.g. Baryaeva. Kondratieva, 2013]. For example, for the prevention of graphic dyscalculia, the development of spatial gnosis is necessary. For this purpose, it is important to refer to the basics of the childs's mastery of the verbal frame of reference in the main spatial directions: forward and backward; up down; to the right - to the left, etc. Of the three paired groups of main directions corresponding to different axes of the human body (frontal, horizontal and sagittal), the upper one stands out first, due to the vertical position of the child's body. This is the beginning of speech therapy work. Then there is the identification of the lower direction, as the opposite side, the vertical axis, and the differentiation of paired groups of directions. The role of the one who is analyzing the movements is exceptionally large. First, children should be taught to use the pointer movement of the hand in the right direction. Further, this gesture will be replaced by less noticeable hand movements. They are replaced by the movement of the head, finally, the children use only the look. So from the practical method of (effective) spatial orientation, children gradually move to another method, which is based on a visual assessment of the spatial distribution of objects.

The sequence of work on the development of preschool children and the correction of spatial orientation disorders in younger schoolchildren should include: orientation on oneself, mastering the scheme of own body; orientation on external objects, the identification and selection of various sides of objects: front, rear, top, side, etc .; the development and application of the verbal frame of reference based on the definition of the spatial direction: down - up, forward - back, right - left, that is, directions along the sides; determining the location of objects in space; definition of own position in space; determining the spatial location of objects relative to each other; determining the spatial location of objects when oriented on a plane, i.e., in two-dimensional space.

For the prevention of dyslexic dyscalculia, it is necessary to select tasks aimed at the formation of a visual image of mathematical signs, geometric figures; formation of understanding of mathematical signs and reflection of understanding in speech activity; the development of perception of colors, shapes, sizes, quantitative representations, ideas about the image of numbers and mathematical signs; development of visual and auditory memory; development of analytical and synthetic activities; the ability to use symbolism; understanding of mathematical terminology, corresponding to the age and the basic content of mathematical development.

The treatment of verbal dyscalculia includes: development in the impressive and expressive speech of words denoting quantitative generalizations and attitudes ("little – much", "more – less"); developing of words denoting opposing actions (like for addition and subtraction), as well as awareness of the differences between actions and denoting; development of words characterizing subject size, and so on.

In one-on-one teaching important is not only the methodology, but also the attitude. It is suggested to apply a step-by-step scheme for developing computational skills on a favorable emotional background with an emphasis on the social significance of the knowledge and skills obtained. In the situation of knowledge testing (control and independent work), children with dyscalculia should be provided with additional time in the amount of 20-25% of the planned for calculations and problem solving, the condition of which is the need to keep intermediate results in memory [Gribanov, Rysina, 2011].

It should also be noted, that a confident step forward was made with the implementation of computer-assisted intervention CAI [Geary, 2012]. The learning outcomes of the Rescue Calcularis computer program are manifested in the form of modulations of brain functions. 5 weeks after the end of classes in children with developmental dyscalculia, there was a significant increase in the activity of the parietal areas of the brain. The Number Race and Graphogame-Math helped kindergarten children with reduced mathematical abilities to develop ability to compare numbers [Geary, 2012].

References

1. Brian Butterworth, Sashank Varma, Diana Laurillard. Dyscalculia: From Brain to Education. *Science* 27 May 2011: Vol. 332, Issue 6033, pp. 1049-1053, DOI: 10.1126/science.1201536
2. Pushpendra Singh. Dyscalculia – a learning disability. IRJMSH Vol 7 Issue 2 [Year 2016]
3. Dénes Szűcs, Usha Goswami. Developmantal Dyscalculia: Fresh Perspectives. Trends in Neuroscience and Education 2 (2013) 33-37
4. Christina B. Young, Sarah S. Wu and Vinod Menon. The Neurodevelopmental Basis of Math Anxiety. Psychological Science OnlineFirst, March, 20, 2012, sagepub.com/journalsPermissions.nav, DOI: 10.1177/0956797611429134, http://pss.sagepub.com.
5. De Nigris, Anna & Masciarelli, Giovanni & Guariglia, Cecilia. (2019). Efficacy of neuropsychological rehabilitation on numerical and calculation abilities: A developmental case study. Applied Neuropsychology: Child. 1-11. 10.1080/21622965.2018.1553044.
6. Chambrier, Anne-Françoise. (2018). Arithmetic skills in children with dyscalculia. ANAE - Approche Neuropsychologique des Apprentissages chez l'Enfant. 30. 596-602.
7. Garcia-Camba, Maria & Garcia Planas, Maria Isabel. (2018). Dyscalculia, mind, calculating brain and education. 480-489. 10.21125/edulearn.2018.0203.
8. Mathematical Cognition Deficits in Children With Learning Disabilities and Persistent Low Achievement: A Five Year Prospective Study / Geary David C. [et al.] // Journal of Educational Psychology. 2012. Vol. 104. № 1. P. 206–223. doi: 10.1037/a0025398.

9. Kosc, L. (1974). Developmental Dyscalculia. *Journal of Learning Disabilities, 7*(3), 164–177. https://doi.org/10.1177/002221947400700309
10. Zafra, Esmeralda. Helping Children with Dyscalculia: A Teaching Programme with three Primary School Children. Procedia - Social and Behavioral Sciences, Volume 191, 2 June 2015, Pages 1178-1182
11. L. B. Baryaeva, S. Yu. Kondratieva. Dyscalculia in children: prevention and correction of disorders and mastery of counting activity MCNIP, Kirov, 2013. ISBN 978-5-906223-45-6
12. Ermolova T.V., Ponomareva V.V., Florova N.B. Dyscalculia in children as a systemic problem of education Journal of Modern Foreign Psychology 2016. Vol. 5, no. 3, pp. 7—27.
13. L.A. Kairova / Correctional developmental technologies in mathematics. Manual /. - Barnaul: AltGPU, 2016. ISBN, 978-5-88210-833-4.
14. Anatoly Gribanov, Natalia Rysina. Behavioral Response of Children with Dyscalculia. Human Ecology, 2011, №3. p.56-60.
15. Larisa Selkina, Yulia Krasilnikova. To the question of diagnostics of discalculia in pupils of the initial classes of the general educational school. Perm Pedagogical Journal, 2015 (5).

YOUR KNOWLEDGE HAS VALUE

- We will publish your bachelor's and master's thesis, essays and papers

- Your own eBook and book - sold worldwide in all relevant shops

- Earn money with each sale

Upload your text at www.GRIN.com and publish for free